MW01156386

This book belongs to

COBWEB THE CAT

a collection of short stories

Copyright © 2012, 2010 by All About® Learning Press, Inc.
Printed in the United States of America

All About® Learning Press, Inc.
615 Commerce Loop
Eagle River, WI 54521

v. 1.2

ISBN 978-1-935197-03-4

Cover Design and Page Layout: David LaTulippe

Stories:
 Marie Rippel: "Fun at the Pond" – "The Nap" – "Fast Fun" – "Off We Go!"

 Renee LaTulippe: "The Pet Duck" – "The Bat and King Sam" – "Frank Shrank!"
          "Cobweb the Cat" – "Ten Wishes" – "At Camp"

Illustrations:
 Donna Goeddaeus: "Fun at the Pond" – "The Nap" – "At Camp" – "Off We Go!"

 David LaTulippe: "The Pet Duck" – "The Bat and King Sam" – "Frank Shrank!"
          "Cobweb the Cat" – "Ten Wishes" – "Fast Fun"

Cobweb the Cat: a collection of short stories is part of the *All About® Reading* program. For more books in this series, go to www.AllAboutReading.com.

To the reader –
may you find yourself among friends

Contents

Fun at the Pond

9

Jill held a wet frog.

Jill set the frog

in the damp sand.

Hop, hop, hop.
The frog went back
to the pond.

The frog swam
past a fish to a pad.

The frog got on top of the pad
to bask in the sun.

A bug went past his pad.

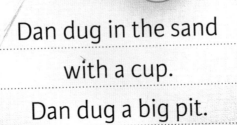

Dan dug in the sand
with a cup.
Dan dug a big pit.

Ben sat in the sand pit.

Dan and Jill fill the pit
with lots of sand.
Ben is still in it!

Did Ben get stuck in the sand?

No!

His leg and hand pop up!

Ben got up with a grin.
Ben had a plan to fish
off of the raft.

Dan ran and got a net,

and Jill got a stick.

The kids sat on the raft.

Sh!

Ben can spot a fish.

"That is not a fish," said Dan.

It fled to the log.

It was quick.

It dug in the mud and muck,

and then it hid.

"A trip to the pond
is fun," said Jill.

The End

The Nap

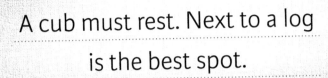

A cub must rest. Next to a log
is the best spot.

The cub is glad to nap.

A big web is spun.

A finch sits on its nest.

A red fox ran to his den...

...and the cub went on
with his nap.

A moth went past, then six.

A wet frog got on top
of the log.

A bug lost its grip on a twig.

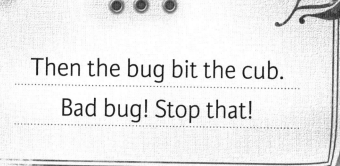

Then the bug bit the cub.

Bad bug! Stop that!

And that was the end
of the nap.

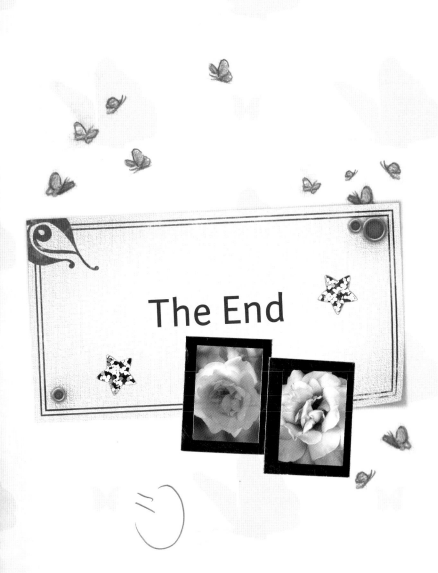

The End

At Camp

Ken and Jack
went up the hill to camp.

"Is that a fox?" said Jack.

It is!

A red fox is on the path!

The sun was hot.

Jack sat in the grass to rest.

Ken set up the tent.
The red fox had a plan
and was in no rush.

Can Jack get a fish
in the pond?

Yes!

The fish fell off the dish!

Thud!

The fox can smell it.

The fox ran off with the fish.

Get him!

The fish is lost,
but Ken has a plums
in his pack.

Not bad!

Ken and Jack had a can of pop,
then went to bed.

Ken and Jack zip up the tent.

It is fun to camp on a hill.

The End

The Pet Duck

Pam has a pet duck
with a black hat.

Rick is a fun duck
but a bad duck!

This duck is quick
and can dash fast
in the grass!

Rick can flip and spin.

Pam is still wet!

The pet duck can sled
on a hill.

And Rick the duck
can swim in a well.

Rick can grab a soft doll

with his bill

if he is glad.

Rick can kick a rock
if he gets mad.

At six on the dot,

Rick will quack and quack.

This duck will not stop!

Then Pam will get him

a snack — a bit of jam

and a glass of milk!

At last, the duck has
a nap with Pam.

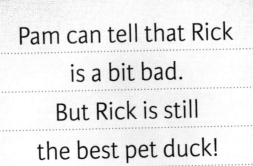

Pam can tell that Rick
is a bit bad.
But Rick is still
the best pet duck!

The End

The Bat and
King Sam

King Sam is the last man
on this cliff. It is just him
and the wind!

His dog and his hen ran off.

His pig and his ox left.

The king is such a sad man.

King Sam just sits
by the dim lamp
and sobs. Sniff!

But then...is that a wing?

It *is* a wing! It is a thin bat!

The bat hung on a twig.

This bat is lost!

"Is that a soft hum?"

said King Sam.

Yes! This bat can sing!

The lost bat sang
a long song. At the end,
the bat got a big hug...
and a big snack!

King Sam has a plan.

The bat will swing on his twig.

King Sam will ring a bell,

and the bat will sing a song.

Then the bat will get a snack!

It is not just the king and the wind.
The bat is fed a lot,
and King Sam has a pal!

The End

Frank Shrank!

Is that a glass of pink milk

on the desk in the den?

Yum! Frank drank it.

Such fun Frank had!

Frank hung on a mug...

...and fell in a drop of pop.

Fizz!

A map led Frank
on a long path,
but Frank did not get lost.

At the end of the map is a web.

Such luck!

Frank can swing on the thick web.

Then Frank slid on a stick.

It is fun to zip

past the lamp

on the back of a moth.

Honk, honk!

The wind of the fan is fast.

Crash!

Frank fell off the moth!

Thud! Frank sank

in a soft pad of ink.

"It is fun to shrink,"
said Frank, "but I think
I must drink that last drop
of pink milk."

Frank is big!

Frank is glad.

The End

Cobweb the Cat

This is Cobweb the Cat.

And this is his windmill
upon the hilltop.

This is a rug for his bed,
but Cobweb cannot nap.

At six, Cobweb had to check the milk that the milkman left.

Then Cobweb had to fix
the bathtub.

Next, Cobweb had to dust the desktop.

Cobweb then fed a snack
to his pet catfish...

...and had a drumstick
and a bit of catnip
for himself!

When the sun got hot,
Cobweb went to sit
with his best pal the bobcat.

Then Cobweb had to hang
his wet rug in the sun.

Next, Cobweb must hunt.
Is that a wing?

Jump!

Got it!

At sunset, Cobweb sang
a song with the bobcat
and the catfish.

And at ten, Cobweb went to bed on his rug. Cobweb can nap!

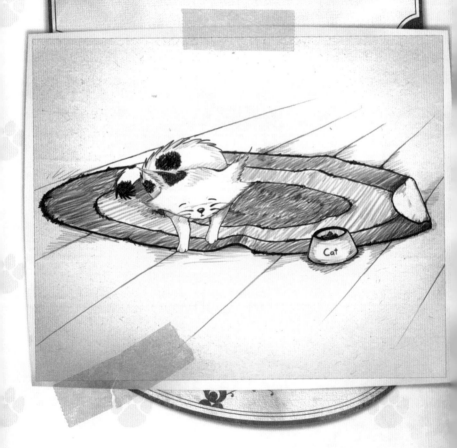

The End

Ten Wishes

Ten kids ring the bell
to wish the king well.
The king was glad.

The king said, "I think ten kids
shall get ten wishes!"

Ted gets soft pups
in cups.

Pam picks an ox

with ten big clocks.

Ben asks for dishes
for his fishes.

Meg begs for fat rats
with such fun hats!

Bob asks for masks

for the bugs in his rugs.

Kim gets thin pigs
that flip upon twigs.

Rick picks trucks of ducks
with lots of spots.

Deb shall get dogs
that spin on logs.

Ken begs for cats

with the wings of bats.

Beth shall get
boxes of foxes
that sing sad songs.

The ten kids
thank the king
for the gifts!
The king gets a hug.

The End

Fast Fun!

Pink pigs pick plums.

Dogs dust
with dishcloths.

Fast frogs flip-flop.

Rams rub red rocks.

Sell six shells.

Duck dresses drip.

Kim kisses Ken.

Tom trip-traps on tracks.

Twin trucks tip.

The End

LOVE
YA

Off We Go!

"I wish we had a sled," Dan said.

"Shall we go to the shed?
I think the shed has
a lot of things in it," said Jill.

"Can this rug be a sled?"

"No."

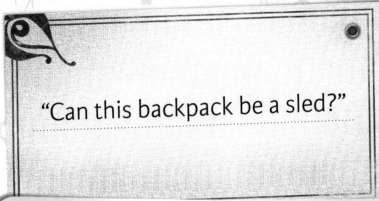

"Can this backpack be a sled?"

"No."

146

"Hmm. A tent, a fan,
a red truck. But no sled."

147

"This will be best. We can sit in this big box top," said Jill.

"I will fix it up
so we can sled in it,"
said Dan.

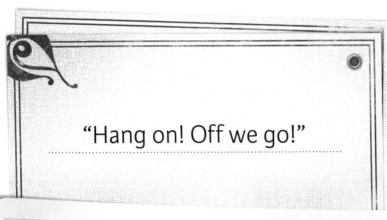

"Hang on! Off we go!"

The sled went so fast! Jill, Dan, and Ben sped past the shed.

No!

A bump!

Slip!

Spin!

Flip!

Crash!

Thud!

"The box top sled is fun!" said Dan.

He and Jill got up to brush off.

"Lend me a hand so we can go back up the hill," said Dan.

And off went Jill, Dan, and Ben.

The End

What?! You're done?

Go on to *What Am I?*

for even more fun!